CW00794756

JUST the TIP

SEX TIPS FOR CHICKS

BY GAY DUDES

LOST
THE
PLOT

LOST
THE
PLOT

A Lost the Plot Book, First published in 2017 by Pantera Press Pty Limited
www.PanteraPress.com

This book is copyright, and all rights are reserved.
Text copyright © Pantera Press, 2017
Created by Ali Green

Design and typography copyright © Pantera Press Pty Limited, 2017

Pantera Press, the three-slashed colophon device, *great storytelling*, *good books doing good things*, *a great new home for Australia's next generation of best-loved authors*, Lost the Plot, WHY vs WHY, *and making sense of everything* are trademarks of Pantera Press Pty Limited.

We welcome your support of the author's rights, so please only buy authorised editions.

Without the publisher's prior written permission, and without limiting the rights reserved under copyright, none of this book may be scanned, reproduced, stored in, uploaded to or introduced into a retrieval or distribution system, including the internet, or transmitted, copied, or made available in any form or by any means (including digital, electronic, mechanical, photocopying, sound or audio recording, or text-to-voice). This book is sold subject to the condition that it shall not, by way of trade or otherwise, be lent, re-sold, hired out, or otherwise circulated in any form of binding or cover other than that in which it is published and without a similar condition being imposed on the subsequent recipient.

Please send all permission queries to:
Pantera Press, P.O. Box 1989 Neutral Bay, NSW 2089 Australia or info@PanteraPress.com

A Cataloguing-in-Publication entry for this book is available
from the National Library of Australia.

ISBN 978-1-921997-98-3 (Hardback)

Cover and Internal Design: Aaron Barnes (Madebya)

Pantera Press policy is to use papers that are natural, renewable and recyclable products made from wood grown in sustainable forests. The logging and manufacturing processes are expected to conform to the environmental regulations of the country of origin.

WE ASKED THE
~~EXPERTS~~ SEXPERTS...

We went directly to the experts[*] on everything "man junk" to bust some myths, get some tips and learn a *lot*.

---

[*] an international panel of gay men ranging in age from early twenties to late thirties

CONTENTS

PREPARATION 101

MASTURBATION: DO IT

It is very hard to pleasure someone who doesn't know what they like and what will get them off.

Alas, there is no magical solution... the only way to find out what you like is to experiment.

Trial and error is key.

So take your pants off, lie back and don't be afraid to use lube. A little goes a long way!

#2

DON'T DO ANYTHING THAT MAKES YOU UNCOMFORTABLE

SAFETY FIRST

- Always wash your hands with soap
- Keep your fingernails clean
- Wash any sex toys before *and* after use, with soap or an antibacterial wash
- Always practise safe sex
- When using a vibrator or dildo it is recommended that you use a condom
- Use lube

#4

START WITH THE CLITORIS

When it comes to masturbation or foreplay use the pad/tip of your index finger to caress your clitoris in a circular motion.

Start out with a gentle pressure, but do experiment with firmer pressures.

You may wish to add your middle finger or a third finger into the mix.

NB. This tip didn't come from a gay man. *Obviously*.

#5

CREATE TENSION WHEN PLEASING YOURSELF OR BEING PLEASURED

Some people do this by:

- Clenching
- Stretching apart their legs
- Holding down one of their legs firmly with their free hand
- Gyrating their hips
- Pushing their clitoris firmly into their fingers or sex toy
- Pressing their whole free hand on their lower abdomen area (just below the bladder)
- Focussing their breathing

#6

FOCUS ON YOUR BREATHING WHEN PLEASING YOURSELF OR BEING PLEASURED

- **Slow it down:** Some people reported that maintaining a consistent, slow and deep, rhythm of breathing heightened their sexual experience by delaying their orgasm and helping to build the pleasurable tension.
- **Create tension:** Others commented that holding their breath for extended periods during the build up worked a treat, and helped speed up the arrival of an orgasm.
- **Do not breath quickly!** Unanimous feedback suggested that short and shallow breathing contributes only to an unsatisfying experience.

#7

TRY MANUAL PENETRATION

Try inserting a finger or two into your vagina, while stimulating your clitoris. Slowly guiding them in and out.

Remember, lube is your friend.

#8

TRY ASSISTED PENETRATION

Experiment with sex toys, to find what you like. There is no "one size fits all" rule.

That said, common recommendations include:

- Powerful and large headed vibrating/massagers to focus on the clitoris
- Full size vibrators that have clitoris stimulator
- Stand alone vibrating devices e.g. bullets or vibrating finger pads

#9

USE A MIRROR TO LOOK AT YOUR VAGINA

Lie down facing a mirror, or use a handheld mirror so that you can clearly see what you're working with.

#10

FIND THE G-SPOT MANUALLY

Lie down on your back. With your palm facing up, insert your index finger (or your index and middle finger) inside your vagina.

The g-spot is located in the upper frontal region of your vagina, about one knuckle deep, so you want to curl your fingers into a "come hither" motion. This may be easier to do with one or both of your legs bent and brought towards your chest.

The g-spot should feel rougher than the rest of your vagina wall.

#11

IF YOU CAN'T FIND THE G-SPOT, TRY AGAIN AFTER YOU'VE ORGASMED

If you cant find the g-spot first time, try to give yourself a clitoral orgasm and then go hunting. The g-spot fills with fluid when aroused making it more sensitive and easier to find post orgasm.

#12

STIMULATE THE G-SPOT

When you have located the g-spot, use a firm "tapping" motion with your crooked finger(s) to the area.

There are also dildos and sex toys designed to specifically stimulate the g-spot. Most are curved to eliminate the guesswork.

WATCH PORN

Specifically, watch porn videos of women masturbating. See the various ways other women masturbate, and give those techniques a go.

Otherwise, watch *amateur* porn. Amateur is the key. Do not watch unrealistic and highly staged videos as they will not help you!

Don't watch *too* much, just enough to see who other people like and do.

Don't let it influence how you have sex, but do let it inspire you.

Watch a variety of porn, including:

- Masturbation
- Hand jobs
- Blow jobs
- Sensual Massage
- 69
- Different Sexual Positions

#14

RECOVERY TIME VARIES

Men reported that it can take them anywhere from 20 minutes to 24 hours to recover after orgasming. It varies from person to person.

It was noted that there is a difference between chemistry and "just fucking someone". Many maintained they could 'keep going' if there was chemistry.

#15

GETTING HARD IS SOMETIMES HARD

The top reasons men reported for being unable to get hard (or maintain an erection):

- Masturbation prior to sexual activity
- Too much exercise that day
- Being tired
- Being stressed
- Not enough nutrients in diet
- Alcohol
- Drug use (prescribed as well as illegal/recreational)
- Lack of attraction to the other person
- Making out with a sloppy kisser
- Being with someone who has poor personal hygiene. *Getting sweaty is fine, but being stinky is not! Take a shower after you've been to the gym.*

#16

IT'S OK IF THERE ARE THINGS YOU DON'T LIKE (EVEN IF OTHER PEOPLE LIKE THEM)

#17

TRY EVERYTHING TWICE

Ok if it's something you ABSOLUTELY hated, then probably leave it as a one-time event. That said, there is reason behind the madness of ensuring you try most things twice.

Often when we try something new we are very focussed on the act itself, and are nervous or awkward.

So once we've given it a whirl, it's a bit less intimidating. Being open to a second attempt means you're much more likely to know if it's something you enjoy.

ETIQUETTE

#18

ALWAYS HAVE TISSUES TO HAND FOR CLEAN UP

#19

HAVE A STASH OF MINTS OR GUM IN YOUR BEDSIDE DRAWER FOR WHEN YOU HAVE OVERNIGHT VISITORS

#20

DON'T EXPECT EVERY PARTNER TO BE KEEN TO KISS FIRST THING IN THE MORNING

#21

SHOWER BEFORE SEX

#22

KEEP YOURSELF TRIM AND CLEAN. GROOMING IS IMPORTANT.

#23

MEN OFTEN WAKE UP WITH AN ERECT PENIS

There are many proposed explanations as to *why* men occasionally wake up with an erection.

Most men we spoke to assumed it was either their body's way of ensuring that they didn't urinate while they were sleeping, as it is very difficult (near impossible) to urinate while you are hard. Or they otherwise assumed that they must have had a sexy dream of sorts.

Regardless, morning wood (as a morning erection is commonly referred to) is occasionally a thing.

Don't be shocked and also don't assume it means the man is 100% DTF (down to fuck).

#24

MAKE NOISE (NOT TOO MUCH)

Silence is awful. You do not want to have to ask "are you having a nice time?" when you're rolling around with someone and vice versa.

Make enough noise so that the person you are with knows you are enjoying yourself. But no need to go over the top... You don't want your neighbours thinking that someone is being murdered in your house.

#25

YOU DO NOT NEED TO SWALLOW SEMEN

When it comes to blow jobs, it is perfectly reasonable not to want to swallow semen.˙

If you would rather spit, keep tissues to hand.

Or if you would prefer they came on you, verbally let them know.

#26

DO NOT EXPECT TO MAKE OUT AFTER SWALLOWING SEMEN

Anecdotally it seems gay men are far more comfortable than straight men about making out with someone immediately after they have swallowed semen.

#27

SPECIFY WHERE SOMEONE SHOULD CUM

Men aren't mind readers. If you don't want him to cum in you (orally, vaginally or anally) let him know and specify where you would like him to cum.

- "Cum on my stomach"
- "Cum on my tits"
- "Don't cum on my face"
- "Cum in this tissue"

#28

TELL HIM "I WANT YOU TO CUM", IT'S HOT AND WILL MAKE HIM CUM FASTER

Many men are awkward about cumming too quickly, so they will often try to hold out for as long as possible.

However, nobody wants lock-jaw or a sandpaper vagina. So when you're done, let him know. He'll likely find it sexy, but also it should do the trick in speeding things up.

#29

THERE IS NO "I" IN TEAM

If it doesn't seem like you partner is ever going to cum, ask "can you finish yourself off?" or "can you help me finish you off".

Alternatively grab their hand, and bring them into the equation non-verbally.

It's not a bad thing if you can't get him off each time.

KISSING

#30

WONDERING WHEN TO MAKE A MOVE? BE AWARE OF BODY LANGUAGE

#31

HAND >> CHEEK/NECK

If things are going well, and you're ready to take charge, step towards the person and place your hand on their cheek or neck (lightly). If they don't move away, pull them in for a kiss.

#32

USE THE LINE "DO YOU WANT TO MAKE OUT?"

If things are going well, ask "Do you want to make out?".

It is straightforward and anecdotally seems to have a close to 100% success rate.

#33

KISS SOFTLY, DON'T GO TOO HARD TOO SOON

#34

DO NOT TRY TO SUCK OR LICK SOMEONE'S FACE. THIS IS NOT HOT

#35

USE TONGUE SPARINGLY

#36

SUCK ON YOUR PARTNERS FINGERS LIKE THEY ARE A PENIS

#37

FOCUS ON THE NECK

The neck is VERY sensitive. Start by kissing the neck downwards from the ear to collarbone, and use tongue (lots of tongue).

#38

NIBBLE THE NECK

Many men noted a bit of nibbling/
biting is welcome, but NO HICKEYS
(This isn't the 90's).

#39

PAY ATTENTION TO THE EAR LOBES

- Nibble the ear lobes
- Lightly lick the ear lobes
- Put the whole ear (or as much of it as possible) in your mouth
- Most men reported they did not like a tongue inside their actual ear (aka a *wet willy*)

#40

PLAY WITH THE NIPPLES

Some men have nipple sensitivity, while others do not. You will be able to tell pretty quickly if they are responsive.

Men who had sensitivity in their nipples reported enjoying having their nipples:

- Licked with the tip of a tongue
- Sucked
- Nibbled
- Gently rubbed with index finger in a circular motion

#41

IF YOUR PARTNER DOES NOT HAVE SENSITIVE NIPPLES, DON'T BOTHER EXPERIMENTING. MOVE ON.

#42

ARM PIT PLAY: DO NOT WEAR DEODORANT

Some men reported enjoying their armpits being kissed/licked. If you are planning on kissing someone's armpits (or would like someone to kiss yours) ensure everyone is recently showered and not wearing deodorant. No one wants a mouth full of *Rexona*.

#43

TOE SUCKING MAY BE A ONE WAY STREET

Most men reported that they would not want to suck someone's toes, however they would be happy for someone to suck their toes.

SPOONING

#44

YOU DON'T HAVE TO BE IN A RELATIONSHIP TO SPOON

Who doesn't love to cuddle?

Most men reported enjoying a post coital spoon, regardless if it was with a one-night stand or a longer-term partner.

There are no sex-pectations.

#45

YOU CAN BE THE BIG SPOON OR THE LITTLE SPOON

There are no set rules.

Many people commented that they regularly switch up positions with longer-term partners.

#46

ENSURE THE BIG SPOON HAS THEIR LOWER ARM IN A COMFORTABLE POSITION

The role of the little spoon is easy.

Generally the little spoon lies on their side and nestles their back against the stomach of the big spoon.

The role of the big spoon requires a little more planning.

Yes, you can easily drape your upper arm around the little spoon. But the lower arm can be a troublemaker.

You don't want to find yourself in an uncomfortable position or with a dead arm that is trapped under your partner or squashed between your stomach and their back.

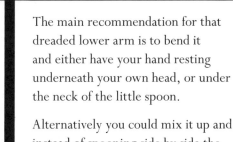

The main recommendation for that dreaded lower arm is to bend it and either have your hand resting underneath your own head, or under the neck of the little spoon.

Alternatively you could mix it up and instead of spooning side by side the big spoon could lie flat on their back, with the little spoon resting their head on the chest of the big spoon.

#47

SPOONING CAN LAST AS LONG AS YOU AND YOUR PARTNER WANT IT TO

Some men reported enjoying sleeping in the spoon position all night long, while other preferred to spoon for between 20 mins to 1 hour and then roll away to sleep.

Remember, you can always start the spoon train back up part way through the night!

THE PENIS

#48

ALCOHOL CAN HAVE A NEGATIVE IMPACT ON GETTING HARD

Whisky dick is a common expression meaning the guy has had too much to drink and can't get hard.

#49

DRUGS CAN HAVE A NEGATIVE IMPACT ON ORGASMS

After consuming Cocaine, people often get *Coke Dick* where they can get it up, but are unable to cum.

#50

DRUGS CAN HAVE A NEGATIVE IMPACT ON PENIS FUNCTIONALITY

"Where has my penis gone?" is a frequent cry of despair from people who are using MDMA and other illicit substances.

#51

TREAT CIRCUMCISED AND UNCIRCUMCISED PENIS' DIFFERENTLY

Uncircumcised penis' are much more sensitive. You should pay attention to the whole penis, whereas with a circumcised penis you are best paying most of your attention to just the head of the penis.

#52

PULL THE FORESKIN BACK ON AN UNCIRCUMCISED PENIS

Start by pulling the skin down enough so that the penis head pops out. Don't pull any more than that without assessing body language.

While most men enjoy the foreskin being pulled back as far as it can go, some men have a tight foreskin and so do not enjoy it.

#53

DURING HAND JOBS, USE LUBE ON A CIRCUMCISED PENIS

#54

NIBBLE THE FORESKIN

Some uncircumcised men like it if you nibble their foreskin (gently).

#55

PLAY WITH THE FORESKIN WHEN GUIDED TO

Some uncircumcised men reported enjoying their foreskin being pulled up and over the head of their penis and played with.

If a man enjoys it, he will let you know. So wait until you are guided or asked to do so.

#56

THERE IS NO 'NORMAL' SHAPE

Penis' come in all different shapes and sizes. Some are straight, some are curved upwards or outwards. Some are thick, some are long.

#57

ADAPT FOR SHAPE AND SIZE

The shape of a penis affects how you would approach various sexual activities including blow jobs and sexual positions.

There is no "right" position, move around until you think it is a good fit or angle.

#58

ADJUST YOUR APPROACH FOR BLOW JOBS

Move your body so you're at the same angle as the penis, allowing it to easily go down your throat.

If the penis is quite curved you may need to approach it side on, or while lying down underneath the man.

HAND JOBS

#59

"I HAVEN'T GIVEN A HAND JOB SINCE I WAS LIKE 14"

Most men reported that hand jobs were not a common part of their repertoire, although jerking someone (without a happy ending) as a warm up for a blow job or sex was fine.

#60

DON'T BE DELICATE. IT'S A WASTE OF TIME

A good amount of firm squeezing of the shaft is recommended.

#61

A GOOD HAND JOB IS GREAT, BUT IT IS HARD TO DO WELL

Most men commented that while they love a GOOD hand job, it is really hard for someone else to be able to do it as good (or better) than they can do on themselves.

#62

TWIST YOUR HAND SLIGHTLY ON THE SHAFT AT THE END OF YOUR UPWARDS MOTION

#63

FOCUS ON THE TIP OF THE PENIS

#64

MUTUAL MASTURBATION IS FUN

Giving your partner a hand job while they finger you at the same time can be a very fun experience.

Try lying down next to each other, so that you are both in a position where you can easily access each other's genitalia.

You may need to try a few positions to ensure neither of your arms are blocking the other persons access.

#65

MASTURBATING AT THE SAME TIME IS HOT

Many men reported that they enjoy the simple act of jerking themselves off, while watching their partner do the same thing.

BALLS

#66

BLOW ON THE BALLS

Gently blow on the balls. This builds anticipation especially if it is before you touch any other part of his genitalia.

#67

TOUCH THE BALLS, LIGHTLY

Before doing anything else, gently touch the balls with your fingertips. You may not even need to touch the balls themselves, you could gently run your fingers over the hair on the balls.

#68

DON'T IGNORE THE BALLS DURING A BLOW JOB

To increase the build of pleasure, take a break part way through a blowjob and focus on the balls.

#69

IF THEY DON'T RESPOND TO BALL PLAY, DON'T GO BACK

If the man is unresponsive when you focus on his balls, don't bother. It's not for everyone.

#70

PUT HIS BALLS IN YOUR MOUTH

Put them in and around your mouth.
One at a time, or both at once
(depends how big your mouth is).

#71

JERK HIM OFF WHILE HIS BALLS ARE IN YOUR MOUTH

GENTLY TUG THE BALLS

Put your hand around each ball and pull down a little bit (starting out gently).

You can tell by your partners reaction if they like it. If so, pull down a little more firmly.

#73

BLOW ON THE BALLS AFTER THEY HAVE BEEN IN YOUR MOUTH

When the balls are still a bit wet from being in your mouth, gently blow on them.

#74

GENTLY SUCK THE BALLS

Suck each ball, but only gently. If you are too firm the sensation can quickly go from amazing to "I've been kicked in the balls". Balls are very sensitive.

#75

A LARGER BALL SACK IS MORE SENSITIVE THAN A SMALLER BALL SACK

BLOW JOBS

#76

MAKE EYE
CONTACT

#77

USE YOUR HAND AND YOUR MOUTH

While it is really nice to have a mouth focus on the whole penis, it is unrealistic to expect someone to sustain that for the duration of an entire blow job.

Use your hand and mouth in partnership, with your hand focussing on the shaft and your mouth on the head of the penis.

#78

YOUR HAND AND MOUTH SHOULD 'KISS' IN THE MIDDLE OF THE PENIS SHAFT

Many make the mistake that when their hand goes up the shaft of the penis towards the penis head, that their mouth should also move upwards off the penis.

However most men reported that it feels better if the mouth and hand work in opposite motions, so that they continually meet in the middle of the shaft.

#79

USE YOUR TONGUE WHEN GOING DOWN AND UP THE PENIS

#80

APPLY FIRM PRESSURE ABOVE THE BASE OF THE PENIS. THIS WILL MAKE HIM CUM FASTER AND MORE INTENSELY.

When the blow job is underway, and you think your partner is getting closer to the point of no return, place your hand above the base of his penis (just underneath their bladder).

Press firmly and rub back and forth like you are massaging that spot.

This will really intensify things and make them blow harder.

#81

DON'T BE TOO GENTLE

#82

DEEP THROATING ISN'T FOR EVERYONE

If you can't get the whole penis in to your mouth, that is OK.

Use your hand and mouth together. That way the whole penis is still being touched.

#83

WHEN ATTEMPTING TO DEEP THROAT, RELAX

#84

WHEN ATTEMPTING TO DEEP THROAT, REPEAT TO YOURSELF "DON'T GAG, DON'T GAG, DON'T GAG"

#85

BLOW JOBS ARE A PROCESS. SO HAVE A CYCLE.

Many men commented how great it is to mix things up – so that you're not doing the same thing all the time (or too many things at the one time).

For example,

1. one could start by licking the balls
2. and then giving a hand job while still licking the balls
3. Soon after that, put the whole penis in your mouth
4. eventually add your hand into the mix with your hand and mouth meeting in the middle of the shaft
5. Rinse and repeat. *By that we mean, start over again… go back to licking the balls.*

#86

IF YOU FIND YOURSELF ON YOUR KNEES, KNEEL ON A PILLOW

#87

THE HARDER THE BETTER

#88

SPEED UP TOWARDS THE CLIMAX

#89

TEASE. SPEED UP AND THEN SLOW DOWN

#90

YOUR SPEED WILL EFFECT HOW MUCH THE MAN WILL BLOW

A harder or faster blow job can result in a more intense orgasm.

#91

NON-VERBAL FEEDBACK IS GOOD

One suggestion, if you are comfortable, is to grab your partners hands and place them on your head while you are mid blow job. This will act as a guiding light to help them show you their ideal rhythm/speed.

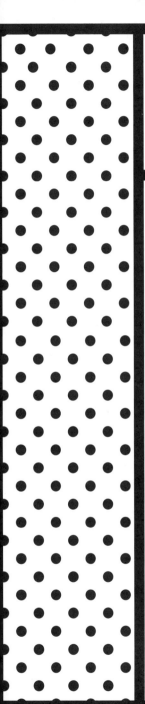

#92

GIVE HIM A HUMMER

It is as simple as it sounds. While you are giving your partner a blow job, hum.

Unless you want a good laugh, it's probably best to avoid humming an actual song. It is suggested you make a "hmmmmmm" noise while your partners penis is in your mouth.

The vibrations from this will send tingly vibrations down his shaft.

It was reported that lower pitch humming created slower vibrations while higher pitch humming creates faster one. And if you really want to intensify the feeling, focus on the head of the penis as the vibrations are most intense right at the opening of your mouth.

NB. It isn't suggested you keep this up for the entire blow job, but certainly add it to your repertoire of licking, sucking and ball play.

THE PERINEUM

#93

THE PERINEUM IS THE PATCH OF SKIN LOCATED BETWEEN THE BASE OF THE BALLS AND THE ASSHOLE

#94

TAP THE PERINEUM FIRMLY WITH TWO FINGERS, WHILE YOU'RE GIVING HEAD TO BRING YOUR PARTNER CLOSER TO CLIMAX.

Many men also reported being aroused when their partner rubbed the area in a circular motion with their fingers.

#95

IF YOU'RE SUPER COORDINATED WHILE GIVING HEAD, THEN MULTITASK

Try to push on the perineum with one hand, while the other hand is doing **#80** by massaging the area just under the bladder.

#96

LICK THE PERINEUM IN CIRCLES OR IN AN UP/DOWN MOTION. ANYTHING GOES.

BUTT PLAY

#97

IT'S EASY TO TELL IF SOMEONE IS INTO BUTT PLAY

You can tell quickly if someone is interested in butt play.

Place your fingers on their perineum, if they pull away – stop right there. If not, slowly work your fingers towards the asshole and gauge the situation.

If they tense up, pull back.

#98

BEFORE ANY BUTT PLAY MAKE SURE YOUR PARTNER HAS SHOWERED AND THOROUGHLY CLEANED THEIR BOTTOM WITH SOAP

#99

USE LUBE (OR SPIT) ON YOUR FINGERS BEFORE GOING ANYWHERE NEAR THE BUTTHOLE

#100

KEEP YOUR FINGER NAILS SHORT WHEN IT COMES TO BUTT PLAY

#101

RIM THE BUTT HOLE

Rimming is when you lick the rim/edge of the butthole.

#102

A MIX OF FINGERS AND TONGUE AROUND THE BUTT HOLE FEELS GOOD.

A circular motion around the rim is a Great Starting Point

#103

WHEN RIMMING, JERK YOUR PARTNER OFF AT THE SAME TIME

#104

WORK FROM BACK TO FRONT AND REVERSE

When rimming the butthole pause your activity and slowly make your way back towards the balls and penis and paying them attention before you head back to the butthole.

#105

GENTLE BLOWING ON THE BUTTHOLE FEELS NICE

#106

IF YOU ARE UP FOR BUTT PLAY, SHOW YOUR PARTNER WHAT YOU LIKE (ON THEM) OR GUIDE THEM ON YOU.

Or give them this sex tips book ;)

#107

IT'S OK TO INSERT A FINGER

Before you consider inserting a finger into the butt hole, make sure you rim the area for a long time to warm it up.

Then start by using your finger to also circle the rim of the hole.

If there is no resistance, slowly start to insert the finger into the hole. SLOWLY.

#108

IF YOU INSERT YOUR FINGERS INTO THE BUTTHOLE, BE CAREFUL AROUND THE PROSTATE

The prostate gland is located about two knuckles deep, against the anal wall.

You should rub it in circles gently, or brush past it with your fingers.

Same goes for a sex toy.

If you are using a sex toy on your partner, make sure it is a longer device, as a longer phallus shape will rub against the prostate as it goes past but a smaller device may poke into the actual prostate which hurts.

SEX

#109

ALWAYS PRACTISE SAFE SEX

#110

GET REGULAR STI CHECKS, IDEALLY ONCE A YEAR

#111

IF THE CONDOM BREAKS, DON'T PANIC

But do go see your pharmacist ASAP (ideally within 12 hours) and ensure you get to your doctor or health clinic for an STI check.

#112

BE RELAXED

#113

SEXUAL CHEMISTRY IS IMPORTANT... PERSONALITY CHEMISTRY MAKES SEX EVEN BETTER

#114

PUTTING ON A CONDOM DOESN'T HAVE TO BE AN INTERRUPTION

Many men commented that their least favourite part of having sex was interrupting the shenanigans to find a condom and then put it on.

Several men flagged anxiety about loosing their erection during this process.

One favourited suggestion was that putting on the condom doesn't need to be a solo act.

Instead of becoming a bit of a clinical act, it's nice, if it's possible, to maintain the sexy fun.

A few suggestions:

- While the man is opening the condom sachet, their partner could stroke his penis with their hand or mouth
- Alternatively you could open the condom and put it on your partner. Unrolling a condom with your hand, or even your mouth is ultra sexy and not as complicated as it may sound.

#115

PUTTING A CONDOM ON SOMEONE ELSE (OR A SEX TOY) ISN'T DIFFICULT

Once you've opened the condom sachet (being careful not to tear the condom in the process), hold the very tip of the condom between your thumb and index finger – this removes any air.

While still holding the tip of the condom, place it on the tip of the penis and using your other hand gently and slowly roll the condom down over the head of the penis and the entire shaft so that it unrolls all the way to the base of the erect penis.

If the condom doesn't roll down the shaft easily, you may have put it on upside down.

A condom only unrolls one way.

If you have done this, dispose of the condom (as it may now have pre-cum on it) and start again with a new condom.

#116

A CONDOM ONLY ROLLS ONE WAY

Attempting to put a condom on the wrong way is a common and very easy to make mistake (especially when your mind might be focussed on other more exciting things, like the naked person in front of you).

That said, it is relatively easy to tell which way a condom rolls if you concentrate on the task for a few seconds.

The roll (what looks like a ring around the condom) should be on the outside of the penis, not touching the shaft. That said, if you're still not sure, a fail safe way to check is if you slightly unroll the condom before it is in contact with the penis.

#117

ADDING A DROP OF LUBRICANT TO THE TIP OF THE PENIS BEFORE PUTTING ON A CONDOM CAN INCREASE PLEASURE FOR THE CONDOM WEARER

#118

ONLY USE WATER OR SILICONE BASED LUBRICANTS DESIGNED FOR USE WITH CONDOMS

Make sure you use a lubricant specifically designed for sex with condoms.

Oil based lubricants and petroleum jelly's can eat through latex (most condoms are made of latex).

Not to mention using something, like a moisturiser, that is not specifically designed for sexual activity, could cause urinary tract infections or inflamations.

#119

AVOID MENTHOL LUBE AND CONDOMS. IT STINGS

#120

FLAVOURED CONDOMS MIGHT SOUND APPEALING, BUT THEY OFTEN HAVE A HIDEOUS TASTE/SMELL

#121

MOVE YOUR BODIES SO THE PENIS PUSHES INTO THE VAGINA AND THEN PULLS PARTLY OUT AGAIN

Do what feels good. But essentially, once the Penis has been guided into the vagina, move one or both of your bodies (depending on the position) so that the Penis is *partly* pulled out of the vagina and can then be pushed back in. Moving your entire body is counter productive, just use your hips. Repeat this so that the thrusting in and out motion becomes rhythmic. Starting out slowly and gently is a good idea, to ensure that both people are comfortable and in a position where it feels pleasurable.

#122

THERE ARE LOTS OF SEXUAL POSITIONS, DO SOME RESEARCH

There are many online and print resources detailing a plethora of sexual positions including "how-tos" and diagrams. Don't be afraid to look them up and see if any look appealing.

Some of the favourite positions reported to us were:

- *Missionary Style:* The woman lies on her back with the man lying face down on top of her between her legs. You may wish to bend your knees, or even wrap one or both of your legs around his back (above his butt).
- *Cowgirl:* The man lies on his back with his knees bent. The woman kneels on top of him. His chest is a good place to rest your hands, and to use as a surface to push

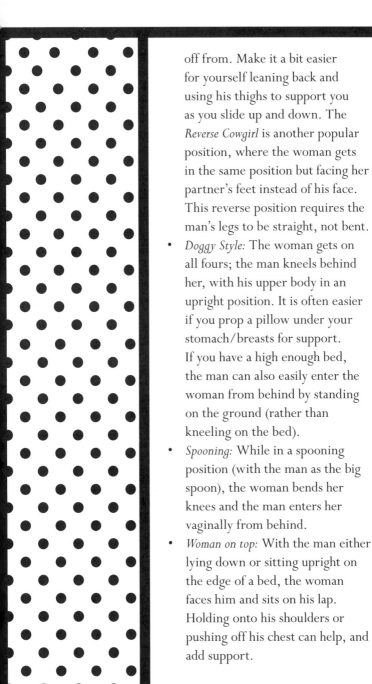

off from. Make it a bit easier
for yourself leaning back and
using his thighs to support you
as you slide up and down. The
Reverse Cowgirl is another popular
position, where the woman gets
in the same position but facing her
partner's feet instead of his face.
This reverse position requires the
man's legs to be straight, not bent.

- *Doggy Style:* The woman gets on
all fours; the man kneels behind
her, with his upper body in an
upright position. It is often easier
if you prop a pillow under your
stomach/breasts for support.
If you have a high enough bed,
the man can also easily enter the
woman from behind by standing
on the ground (rather than
kneeling on the bed).

- *Spooning:* While in a spooning
position (with the man as the big
spoon), the woman bends her
knees and the man enters her
vaginally from behind.

- *Woman on top:* With the man either
lying down or sitting upright on
the edge of a bed, the woman
faces him and sits on his lap.
Holding onto his shoulders or
pushing off his chest can help, and
add support.

#123

WHEN IT COMES TO SEXUAL POSITIONS, BE REALISTIC

If you're not an Olympian gymnast there are likely a bunch of positions that will be awkward, uncomfortable or just impossible for you to attempt.

That is fine! Try new things, but know your limits.

#124

THE 'RIGHT' SEXUAL POSITION FOR YOU AND YOUR PARTNER IS DEPENDENT ON MANY FACTORS, INCLUDING: THE HEIGHT OF BOTH PEOPLE, STRENGTH, BALANCE, PENIS CURVE/LENGTH/ GIRTH AND SO ON

What feels great with one partner, may not work with another partner.

For example a penis with a bit of a curve to it may rub the g-spot or the

vaginal walls in a great w[...]
partner, and may awkwardl[...]
another partner making them [...]
less aroused and more like they ne[...]
to pee.

There are countless sexual positions.

So there is no harm in working
out generally what your favourite
positions are, but bear in mind they
may not work as well with a new
partner. It's also fun to try new
things (twice).

ay with one
prod
eel
d

25

YOU DON'T HAVE TO STICK TO THE ONE SEXUAL POSITION DURING ONE SEXUAL SESSION

If it's working for you, then great!

But there is no harm in mixing it up. Men reported that they often enjoyed changing positions up to 2-3 times during a single sexual encounter.

#126

WOMEN VARY IN DEPTH

We often talk about how "size matters" with reference to a penis.

However, women also vary in how deep they are.

A man with an average sized penis may well be able to have his whole penis inside one women's vagina, and with another partner may realise the whole thing doesn't fit.

#127

AVOID COITUS INTERRUPTUS

- Switch the ringer off every nearby phone
- Don't text or look at your phone during sex
- Don't stare at the ceiling & work on your shopping list. Stay in the moment
- In a hotel room, place a 'Do Not Disturb' on the doorknob (unless you are angling for someone from the turn-down service to join in).
- Lock your door if any children are about

#128

IF YOU LIVE WITH HOUSEMATES OR FAMILY, BE CONSIDERATE

Don't scream the house down — perhaps turn on some music (at a moderate decibel level).

#129

AVOID CARPET BURN, IT HURTS

Do not have sexual relations on synthetic rugs. If you find yourself kneeing or lying on a surface that may cause friction change locations or put a pillow or soft towel underneath you.

#130

IF YOU ENJOYED THE SEXUAL EXPERIENCE, TELL YOUR PARTNER

There is nothing like a boost to the ego after some play time between the sheets!

#131

IT'S NOT JUST ABOUT DIFFERENT SEXUAL POSITIONS

A little novelty can be lots of fun.

Consider introducing sex toys into the bedroom, sex games, role-play and more.

You won't know what you and your partner are into unless you try it.

Generally speaking it is recommended you talk about it *before* it happens. Often the element of surprise doesn't work.

#132

SAFETY FIRST: IF YOU HAVE A TRAPEZE, SEX SWING, OR A SIMILAR CONTRAPTION, CHECK THE CONNECTING BOLTS REGULARLY

#133

WATCH YOURSELF HAVING SEX IN A MIRROR

But make sure passers-by can't see the mirror from outside the house, unless you're a show off (or don't mind the police showing up).

#134

IF YOU HAVE A MIRROR ABOVE YOUR BED, KEEP IT SPARKLY CLEAN

#135

GUIDE THE PENIS INSIDE YOUR VAGINA WITH YOUR HAND

Sometimes the vagina can seem a bit like *Aladdin's* cave… full of wonder, but easy to get lost in.

Help a brother out, and when it's time to get down and dirty and have some good old-fashioned sex use your hand to guide (and then insert) the penis into your vagina.

#136

USE VERBAL AND NON-VERBAL CUES TO SIGNIFY WHAT YOU LIKE

Tell your partner what you do and don't like (as it's happening).

Don't shoot off a long shopping list of likes and dislikes, but in the moment reinforce the things you enjoy and if there is something you don't like as much either tell your partner or take charge and change up the position.

#137

CLOSE YOUR BLINDS/ CURTAINS, UNLESS YOU WANT STRANGERS OR NEIGHBOURS TO WATCH

#138

WHEN IT COMES TO PRIVACY, BEWARE OF FROSTED GLASS

You may feel safe with frosted glass windows, however at night time shut those curtains! With an interior light on, frosted glass often appears just as transparent as regular glass.

ANAL SEX

#139

SHOWER FIRST

#140

ALWAYS USE CONDOMS WHEN HAVING ANAL SEX

#141

RELAX, AND MAKE SURE YOUR BUTTHOLE IS ALSO RELAXED

#142

PRACTISE WITH A SEX TOY

It is not recommended that a penis be the very first thing to ever penetrate you anally.

Work up to it.

Start with a finger or a sex toy. You could try this by yourself, or with a partner.

#143

USE LOTS OF LUBE

Make sure there is lube not only on his penis, but also inside your butthole.

You should be the one to lube up the inside of your bum.

#144

POOP A SHORT WHILE BEFORE ANAL (AND CONSIDER DOUCHING TOO)

#145

SIMILARLY TO SEX, ANAL WILL MOST LIKELY HURT AT FIRST

#146

WARM UP THE AREA WITH LOTS OF FINGER PLAY AND RIMMING

#147

INSERT FINGERS FIRST

Make sure your partner inserts his fingers, and plays with you anally to ensure you are comfortable before he inserts his penis.

#148

BE IN CONTROL

The person being penetrated should ideally be in control of the situation, the motion and the pace.

#149

"COWGIRL" IS A GOOD POSITION FOR ANAL SEX

Instruct your partner to lie flat on his back. Sit over the top of him, slowly lowering yourself onto his penis while guiding his penis into your butt.

This way you can control the speed and depth.

#150

THE PENIS MUST BE SUPER HARD TO BE ABLE TO ENTER YOU ANALLY

#151

KEEP BREATHING WHILE ANYTHING IS BEING INSERTED INTO YOUR BUTTHOLE

#152

DO NOT LET HIM PULL OUT QUICKLY

There is a *real* chance you will shit yourself if this happens.

#153

SOMETIMES THERE WILL BE A BIT OF POOP ON THE TIP OF THE CONDOM

When your partner pulls out, it is not uncommon for there to be a tiny bit of poop on the tip of the condom.

Do not panic.

Instead just make sure you take the condom off your partner and put it in the bin.

#154

COMMON FEARS ABOUT ANAL SEX ARE ALL TO DO WITH POOPING YOURSELF OR POOPING AS YOUR PARTNER PULLS OUT

PLAY TIME

#155

HEIGHT IS THE BIGGEST PROBLEM WHEN IT COMES TO THE 69 POSITION. SOMETIMES IT IS JUST NOT POSSIBLE.

#156

SOME PEOPLE LIKE DIRTY TALK. OTHERS HATE IT.

There is only one way to find out what works for you, and you and your partner.

Be yourself.

If you feel like saying some dirty things in the moment – go for it. Your partner may be very aroused, or it may distract them and take them out of the moment.

Many men commented that dirty talk is great in a one night stand, but sometimes harder with a long term partner as it can seem a bit derogatory when the sex is about love not just lust.

#157

ANYTHING IN THE HEAT OF THE MOMENT COULD BE HOT. FOLLOW YOUR INSTINCTS

#158

SHOWER TOGETHER

Before. After. Or, during sex.

A shower together can be fun, and often intimate.

#159

IF YOU LIKE IT A BIT HARDER, LET YOUR PARTNER KNOW

#160

EXPERIMENT WITH HOT AND COLD TEMPERATURES

Ice cube play is fun. Experiment with different temperatures like icecubes, icecream, teas, hot chocolate etc by putting those substances in your mouth before you kiss, suck or lick anywhere on your partners body.

A contrast of cold to warm is good. Although avoid extreme cold when you are putting a penis or balls into your mouth.

You can also find items of different temperatures to rub on your partner's body. E.g. Rubbing an ice cube around a nipple is a popular suggestion.

#161

SEX TOYS CAN BE FUN TO USE WITH A PARTNER. ASK FIRST

#162

BUTT PLUGS AREN'T THERE TO PLUG UP ANAL LEAKAGE, THEY ARE A SEX TOY

#163

BUTT PLUGS ARE DIFFERENT SHAPES TO DILDOS

#164

USE SEX TOYS WITH LONGER TERM PARTNERS, NOT RANDOMS

#165

COCK RINGS ARE HIT AND MISS

A cock ring wraps around the base of the penis, and often they also vibrate. They can be worn during sex.

#166

SEX IN PUBLIC OR SEX WITH SOMEONE WATCHING CAN BE HOT

#167

IT'S SEXY KNOWING YOUR PARTNER ISN'T WEARING UNDERWEAR IN PUBLIC, IT'S SEXIER WHEN THEY TELL YOU

#168

TEST THE WATERS WITH SPANKING

If you like to spank or be spanked, try a gentle test spank to see how your partner reacts.

Alternatively, ask "I like a bit of kink are you ok with that"?

#169

ALWAYS ASK FIRST WHEN IT COMES TO KINKIER ACTIVITIES

Watersports: Most men were OK being peed on (or peeing on someone else) as long as it was neck down, and ideally in the shower.

Choking: Choking is most definitely not for everyone! If you're not keen to be choked or to choke someone, make that very clear if your partner indicates an interest.

Many men reported enjoying a firm to hard hand around the base of their neck during sexual activities. Firm meaning pressure but they were still able to inhale and hard being unable to inhale for short periods of time.

Those men commented:

- Push hard but then back off so there is time to breath properly
- Do not do it all the time, just in parts of sex

Electrode Play: A small sample of men were excited by electrodes. This is where they clamp an electrode to their balls and part goes inside their ass. Or they can be clamped on to their nipples. An electric charge of varying degrees shoots through the electrodes. This is not for everyone.

COMPATIBILITY

#170

FEEL COMFORTABLE GIVING CONSTRUCTIVE FEEDBACK TO ANY PARTNER (REGARDLESS IF THEY ARE A SHORT-TERM OR A LONG-TERM PARTNER)

#171

SEX IS DIALOGUE

You have to listen and respond (to both verbal and non-verbal cues, like body language).

If someone isn't giving you non-verbal or verbal feedback then there is only so much you can do.

#172

DON'T BE AFRAID TO SAY NO

#173

**DON'T BE
NERVOUS TO
SUGGEST NEW
THINGS**

SEXUAL CHEMISTRY IS KEY

Everything is great when you have the right chemistry with someone.

Follow your instincts.

#175

SLEEP COMPATIBILITY IS JUST AS IMPORTANT AS SEX COMPATIBILITY

Great sleep chemistry, with a long term partner, is just as important as sexual chemistry.

By this we mean, that you can sleep soundly and comfortably together.

Like sex, this can take practise and mentally means you need to be very comfortable with the person.

#176

CHEMISTRY. CHEMISTRY. CHEMISTRY. THE 3 C'S ARE WHAT YOU NEED

At the end of the day it all comes down to chemistry.

You don't want to miss out on an awesome person just because you're focused on having a specific type or expectations.

For a long term partner, make sure you have the 3 C's.

1. Sexual chemistry
2. Personality chemistry
3. Sleep chemistry

GOT SOME
EXTRA TIPS?

Email them to
JustTheTip@PanteraPress.com

& your tips might make it into the next edition of

A TIP OF THE HAT TO THE TIPPERS
(ACKNOWLEDGEMENTS)

A big thank you to the many contributors of this book for sharing some VERY personal and HUGELY insightful information and secrets!

Additional special thanks go to:

Loucineh Mardirossian
Christian Valmont
Joshua Flint
Michael Dunn
Peter Michael
Prakul Duggal
Ryan Brailsford
Simon Jobson
William Clifton-Andrews

And to the other special few who wish to remain anonymous.